A Real Shot
At Real Wealth
For The Little Guy!

What If...
It Were Really True?

By
The Eccentric Influencer

A Real Shot At Real Wealth For The Little Guy

The Eccentric Influencer
c/o GreeneLink Consulting
PO Box 698
Flagler Beach, FL 32136
Phone: 386.243.5313
Email: info@theeccentricinfluencer.com
Website: TheEccentricInfluencer.com

ISBN-13: 978-1511504928
ISBN-10: 1511504927

Credits
Prepared for Publication by: Kelly J. Grillo, PhD

First Edition
May, 2016

Table of Contents

What If... It Were Really True?

The Dedication

The very thought of writing this book was daunting - *yet very intriguing*. The thought of **me** writing this book was just plain silly.

If it hadn't been for my loving family and oh-so-patient friends, this work might never have been completed. Even when unattractively pontificating, each who care about me continued to be encouraging and supportive. Set to convince me I had something important to say, they suffered through each and every page with helpful suggestions and the kindest of critiques.

Should only one reader receive any benefit from these words of my heart, the two of us will be forever grateful for their patience and love.

~

I owe special thanks to someone I have never met.

Steve Harrison of Bradley Communications for his ever-so-many motivational, inspirational and encouraging moments... especially those that came like magic when I seemed to have lost my way.

The Pre-Ramble

The descriptions and definitions as defined in this work may stray from and conflict with those of Webster, Wikipedia and other credible and intelligent resources.

Because I can, I boldly, even audaciously take license to coin new words and phrases and, on occasion, will shamelessly use tiresome and overworked clichés.

When it serves my purpose and helps make my point, I will self-servingly modify, adjust and perhaps somewhat redefine customary depictions and characterizations.

If necessary, I will tediously repeat myself and may even alter and expand traditional meanings, explanations, and descriptions.

With all due respect, I am apt to be opinionated and politically incorrect but will most always speak my mind. I will try very hard to keep from being insulting or out-of-line but know full well, every once in a while, I will inevitably be a bit of a bully.

I know it's hard to believe, but I do this with love and caring for my fellow man.

The Eccentric Influencer

The Prologue

Oh, the clarity and the wisdom of hindsight!

Sometimes, yesteryear is a hard place to visit but all of us, at one time or another, will find we are drawn back into the past.

We might find solace in reliving our moments and perhaps confirmation when reevaluating our decisions. Hopefully, we can find closure when revisiting the consequences.

~~

It is as though a thick, smoky veil has parted allowing us to step through; this time a spectator rather than a participant. This time, a presence without a voice.

*What if...*we could again step through, this time taking with us all the knowledge and wisdom borne of our curiosity? Would we thoughtfully weight our options with facts, fully understanding there is little difference between the fear of failure and the fear of success?

*What if...*we had all the answers and solutions uncovered throughout the years by our questions and the many successes funded by out false starts and failures? Would we be less complacent, more courageous, perhaps more willing to take a risk?

*What if...*we could see the possibilities from a different but informed-by-our–past point of view? Would we be less judgmental, more open-minded?

*What if...*we could do it all again? Would we be more deliberate, setting more important goals for the future; not bending to the needs of the now?

*What if...*we could really relive our yesteryear? What would we hope to change?

Chapter One

*"The man
Who has no imagination
Has no wings."*

Muhammad Ali, Athlete

The Perspective

What do we see when we are last in the herd?

In retrospect, long before I learned to listen to understand, I was a member of the herd. One of The Little Guys, I was buried deep in the needs-of-now and the debts-of-the-moment. I eagerly traded weeks and months, even years, for the privilege of a paycheck. I allowed the money-in-my-pocket amount to be predetermined by my handlers and then preempted by the tax collector.

That Was Yesterday!

The 20th Century conformist is led by the masses to live in other people's thinking. Each of our footsteps reflects the traditional career choices set in motion by the prejudices and favoritisms of past generations.

Most of us are *intended* to be conformists; subject to the example set by others. We are preprogrammed to go to school and learn what others want us to learn. The predetermined goal is to get a job and go to work for the system so we can buy a car, then a house and have a credit card or two or five.

From the day we were born, we were groomed for our futures – *for better or worse*. We emulate those who have come before us for they are the only example we see. We are ruled and judged by our parents, our church, our peers, our teachers and our government.

Then, one day, we are set loose, invigorated with other people's thinking. In short order, we find ourselves working for someone else's goals and subject to our government-planned retirements. Each week, we start over at zero.

Maybe, as a bushy-tailed new business owner, we invest what we have and start out in the red. Then, at midnight the first day of every month, we are pre-expensed into debt with upcoming overhead, payroll and a tribute to Uncle Sam. Not at all the American Dream.

If we aren't careful, we can find ourselves just another member of a herd doing things the way they've always been done.

No one cares if we owe more than we earn as long as we pay our taxes as well as the interest on the money we borrow to go deeper in debt. It is of little matter, as long as we are led to believe we have the rest of our lives to pay for the privilege. Worst of all, we continue to replicate, condemning each new generation to do the same.

The rut keeps getting deeper, and we just keep digging.

This Is Today!

Technology is yanking us out of the Industrial Age, hurling us headfirst into the 21st Century; the Age of Information.

Social media and the Internet are rapidly changing the landscape in general. The E-commerce revolution is localizing global merchants, creating a new level of personal opportunity with a neighborhood look and feel.

Suppliers can connect directly to their target market. The 20th Century middleman and retailer are becoming dispensable, costing jobs and shifting bottom line profits. Stand-alone megastores and glitzy malls are downsizing or closing their doors forever.

For richer or poorer, economic profiles are fluctuating and forever changing the game. With each new stride, the economy is transitioning, and traditional consumer/employer/employee relationships are being put to the test.

Today's consumer is much better educated. Internet savvy, they are finding value, variety, and convenience with expanded brand options. Less likely to purchase based simply on brand loyalty, this new-age shopper is discovering alternate ways to compare quality and price. Now a priority, the well-informed are demanding better products of higher quality and more stringent manufacturing standards.

Large and small business employers, constantly pelted with mandated requirements, are watching expenses skyrocket with added employee benefits and the demand for higher wages. As a consequence, bottom lines are finding long-term, full-time employment options with their generous retirement plans impossible to sustain.

The employee, especially *The Little Guy,* is losing ground.

Older employees with adding machine skills are being replaced with the newly-minted techno minds of the young, just out of school.

Technology is redefining traditional job descriptions or erasing them altogether. The familiar work-a-day world is shifting from steady employment to job outsourcing and exporting. Fewer opportunities for growth, stability and longevity are eroding the promise of security in the retirement years. Short-term, temporary off-the-traditional-payroll job options are becoming more the norm.

These options, characterized as *"Alternative Employment Arrangements"* by the United States Department of Labor **http://www.bls.gov/cps/lfcharacteristics.htm** are officially defined as:

- **Independent Contractors:** "Self-employed or wage and salary workers identified as *independent contractors, independent consultants,* or *freelance workers.*"
- **On-call Workers:** "Workers called to work *only* as needed, although they can be scheduled to work for several days or weeks in a row."
- **Temporary Help Agency Workers:** "Workers paid by a temporary help agency, whether or not their job is temporary."
- **Workers Provided by Contract Firms:** "Workers employed by a company that provides them or their services to others under contract; those usually assigned to only one customer and usually work at the customer's worksite."

Common to these "alternative" work choices are erratic and undependable work schedules that produce unstable earnings and restrict company benefits.

Employee/employer contributions to Social Security, healthcare and retirement benefits are sporadic, underfunded or nonexistent.

Employer liability, employee safety, and consumer protection are pretty much a second thought – if given any thought at all.

What about Tomorrow?

Graduating youngsters are excited and apprehensive – no different than those who came before. Their futures are still to be determined; their expectations hopeful but unproven.

Perhaps their generation will be the one that stops the digging?

Caught between the Ages, Millennials, *those born since 1981*, have one foot planted in each century. According to the Pew Research Center **http://pewresearch.org,** this group has *"surpassed Baby Boomers as the nation's largest living generation"* and a big part of the *"79% of the public that says that jobs are difficult to find in their community."*

Young two-paycheck families, are losing interest in climbing over each other on the "ladder", building one-company careers. Seeking the financial means for independence and freedom, they believe quality-of-life balanced with family first should no longer be a back-burner project.

Boomers and grandparents, little more than youngsters themselves, are excited and ready for part two.

Based on the conventional wisdom of financial planners, many have planned to maintain 70% of their current income, finding the sacrifice of the 30% tougher than then thought. The rest are facing tomorrow one day at a time. Still highly productive and more than experienced, they hope to continue to afford the independence they've earned and freedom they value.

The more fortunate of the golden-agers are somewhat content. Although older, they're younger than they expected to be. For others, their financial future is fuzzy and less predictable. Some rely entirely on Social Security, living at poverty level or less; their families working hard to pitch in the rest.

Each generation seems to be walking on shifting sands. Each is dealing with its own economic uncertainties.

Against All Odds

Along with the 20th Century, traditional income opportunities are quickly fading into the past. Financial futures, especially those of *The Little Guy*, are clouded and less certain. Jobs are harder to find and those with a dream to own their own business are in for difficult lessons or already broken and scarred.

According to Forbes, quoting a Bloomberg statistic at **http://www.forbes.com,** *"8 out of 10 entrepreneurs who start businesses fail within the first 18 months. A whopping 80% crash and burn."*

The odds are against *The Little Guy* right from the start.

Chapter Two

"Ever Tried? Ever Failed?
No Matter. Try Again.
Fail Again. Fail Better."

Samuel Beckett 1906-1989
Irish Novelist, Poet

A Different Era

I have vivid memories from long past of others trying to rope me into what I believed was a third-world industry.

I knew very little but had heard its provocative language with words like "pyramids" and "schemes." It spoke of letters that forged chains and touted overnight riches that purchased mansions and yachts. Most, designed by the greedy, had a remarkable reputation for deceiving the gullible and tricking the trusting...and I knew I was neither.

Then one day, purely by chance, I found myself listening to a friend who had listened to a friend... and I was intrigued. Although the language was consistent, I realized there was so much more to learn. I heard myself asking, what if....it were really true? It was then that I set out to uncover the rest of the story.

Not really a third-world industry, the 20th Century Multi-Level Marketing companies, as well as its plethora of relatives, offered an income system to anyone who wanted to make extra money. Some had a level of success but most fell by the wayside.

As the bigger picture came into focus, I concluded their idea was really very good – offering opportunity. It proved to be the product and income delivery systems that were the not-so-good.

Many of these last-century systems are still in place, and others are being developed every day. Most are designed to succeed mainly on corporate profits, but there is a handful deliberately designed to succeed on the success of others.

For this handful, I have coined the term "Systematic Marketing".

Out of the Ashes

Rising from the ashes of the last century, the stunning story of this remarkable industry with 21st Century appeal is its wealth of opportunity entirely within the reach of *The Little Guy*.

Recognize it for what it is... a remarkable industry focused on a trifecta of winning solutions.

- Partnering with companies serious about delivering the best in quality and performance and, as a result, enjoying greater revenue in the bottom line.
- Delivering quality products and services to consumers who deserve value, choices and affordable prices.
- Offering significant income entirely within reach of *The Little Guy*.

By simply tapping into the resources of an established big business system, *everyman* can build-to-own a stable, low-risk, long-term personal asset. Taking the best of its distant relatives, *Multi-Level Marketing,* and *Network Marketing*, the finest Systematic Marketing business models are structured on:

- Value of sought-after products or services
- Delivered through a successful big business system
- Led by credible management with integrity and foresight
- Offering *The Little Guy* a *real* shot at *real* wealth.

The big business partner brings its products as well as the legitimacy and the stability of its system. *The Little Guy* brings the networking and marketing.

When compared to the initial investment in yesterday's business systems, *including the franchising models*, today's Systematic Marketing start-up costs can be minimal with the potential for an *extra*-ordinary upside.

Requiring much of the same business-owner skills and dedication as in traditional business, *and if we have chosen wisely,* it is without risk and liability.

...And just what the hell is wrong with that?

Seeking the Truth

Truth examined with an open mind, *whatever the results*, is a critical element in the very foundation of success...and success leaves clues *if we are listening to learn.*

Taking on the imposters of the last century, Systematic Marketing is bent on exposing their mindless myths and meaningless misunderstandings.

In every instance, knowledge is power!

The Myths: Totally out of sync with reality, many hold the distorted notion Systematic Marketing is illegal or only for those out for the fast buck.

Most have this dismissive attitude only because it is something they *think* they know or what someone has said. Not for the bull-headed or those stuck in musty 20th Century thinking, Systematic Marketing is for those planning their futures based on truth.

"It's a scam!" The Truth: Scams are dishonest schemes set up to part money from its rightful owner. There are unscrupulous people and unethical businesses all over the world positioning themselves to do just that. Legitimate Systematic Marketing business systems offer real products or services to consumers who really *want* them, *need* them and are *willing to pay* for them.

"It's a pyramid scheme!" The Truth: The structure of an organization does not determine legality. If it did, corporations, churches, and the government would all be illegal because they all have a pyramid structure.

"It doesn't work; no one really makes any money!" The Truth: It depends on the business model and it's Compensation Plan.

If we have chosen wisely, the right plan plus individual effort, driven by determination, consistency, and commitment = success.

"I have to badger my friends and family!" The Truth: It's in our nature to share something good; a movie or a restaurant. If we believe we have truly found *A Real Shot at Real Wealth for The Little Guy,* why wouldn't we spread the word?

"Only the guy at the top makes money!" The Truth: This statement is more fitting to those who have a "job" (some <u>J</u>ust <u>O</u>ver <u>B</u>roke). Most likely, a minimum wage worker will never be a President or CEO.

In a *really* good Systematic Marketing company, *The Little Guy begins* at the top at the ready to build a new organization.

"It takes advantage of people!" The Truth: A success-driven Systematic Marketing income model is based on individuals working as a team with a common goal; each helping the other succeed.

What other industry builds on the success of others?

"It's another one of those get-rich-quick schemes!" The Truth: A good Systematic Marketing business is a real business - not a hobby. It is not fast money nor an answer to the needs-of-now.

There are still some dishonorable companies that recruit with hype and hyperbole and more coming to the market every day. Self-education will quickly weed these out, leaving only those opportunities that are viable and worth our time and dedication. As with any legitimate business model, it's not about getting rich quick. It about hard work and dedication; investing time and energy.

I have heard these myths and so many more! My tendency is to want to defend each as a challenge but, in any of these statements, what can I defend? I have no idea what others mean and usually, neither do they. Most are just echoing what they have heard others say. Some just want to share what they think they know.

I have learned to take the time to drill down and ask pointed questions; really paying attention to the answers. Actively listening for the real issues, I welcome the chance to address them specifically.

Frankly, I am flustrated by those who think they know it all and prove, by their lot, they know nothing. They make decisions based on advice from their out-of-work brother-in-law, or the can't-get-out-of-my-own-way neighbor rather than listen to the facts.

Really?

The Misleading: Some business models encourage unrealistic expectations and foster the exaggerated. Overstatements and the embellished are used to create a sense of urgency – just to get the newcomer and their money.

"Get in on the ground floor!" The Truth: This *gotcha* implies we have to act fast because the first in wins and the last in loses.

I am continually puzzled by those who repeat this phrase with enthusiasm, especially to their friends and family, believing it is something splendid. Companies that have built their compensation formulas around this philosophy are betting their income on those they deliberately set up to lose.

How about a company where everyone is standing as an equal with an equal chance, *even if the last to stand*?

"Get in now before the market is saturated!" The Truth: Will the time ever come when every person on earth is buying the same product from the same manufacturer?

"This business will automatically build around you. You don't have to do anything!" The Truth: Great example of hype! If the organization is built around this philosophy, who will do the work? No work, no success – for anyone!

"Become a millionaire overnight!" The Truth: Every real business takes time and dedication to be stable and richly successful.

If you want to get rich quick,
Stop right now
And count your blessings!

Myths and the misleading will always persist about any industry. Common sense dictates we can't let these misconceptions stop us from educating ourselves. The goal is to learn all we can so we can thrive in our own thinking and have a real shot at reaching our personal goals.

Chapter Three

"Real success
Is not determined
By our income
Or our possessions
But by the positive impact
We have
On the lives of others".

The Eccentric Influencer

Taking the Shot!

Systematic Marketing is a powerful process that levels the playing field.

Who's it for?

Tailor-made for *The Little Guy*, Systematic Marketing is a realistic option to supplement an income, develop a Plan B, enrich a retirement program, launch a new business or get out of debt.

It's also for those who realize the chances are slim they will ever have a **rea**l shot at **real** wealth working for others.

Many are not entrepreneurs nor meant to be in business for themselves, and that's ok! But for those who want to be, this industry can offer a remarkably low-investment, low-risk, high-potential income option.

If we have chosen wisely, this new-age commerce system is jam-packed with non-traditional business-owner benefits including:

- Work from home
- Low financial risk
- Unlimited income
- Family first
- Little or no inventory
- Token or no deliveries
- No invoicing or collections
- No employees
- Little or no overhead

- Nominal or no initial investment
- Flexible work schedule
- Low monthly financial requirement

For those committed to working smarter, it can mean freedom from debt and the luxury of choices.

...And just what the hell is wrong with that?

How does it work?

Every successful big business has an established system. Each system is designed, structured, funded, developed and launched with products and services that are market-tested and proven by consumer demand.

Support for these systems requires significant ongoing investment for general overhead, human resources, advertising, sales, marketing, and distribution.

Some old-line big businesses with old-line processes are still stuck in the past. Moving their products through expensive, multi-tiered distribution channels, they spend fortunes on reaching and keeping their customers.

The Systematic Marketing systems are somewhat centered on the same production foundation but differ significantly in their marketing methods to cultivate new customers and promote retention.

An innovative 21st Century **win-win-win** marketing model, Systematic Marketing is based on word-of-mouth; powerful and personal at the same time.

A **winner**, the more forward-thinking enterprises are realizing traditional *paying-before-the-fact-expecting-some-degree-of-success* marketing and advertising is wasteful and counter-productive.

They've discovered, by embracing the Systematic Marketing processes, they can cut overhead and meaningfully increase their bottom-line profit. Now in a better position to compete, they see a highly profitable, less expensive means to expand their customer base. As a result, they can catch their customer's attention face-to-face.

Changing gears, they can redirect a portion of their marketing budget for profit-rich *after-the-sale* results.

A winner, *The Little Guy,* can own a business by accessing a ready-made system and representing that system to the consumer.

As a self-governing, small business CEO, each can perform a variety of services for the big business partner. In exchange for some form of compensation, services offered directly to the consumer might include some level of distribution, marketing, sales, product delivery, collections and customer service.

For the most part, *The Little Guy* has a huge financial opportunity by creating teams of other CEOs and duplicating the win. Rewards are earned by leveraging time and effort, building on the accomplishments of others. Investment is minimal, risk is pretty much eliminated, and potential is unlimited.

As a product or services representative, *The Little Guy* is compensated by the Big Business partner to:

- Interface one-on-one with the consumer on behalf of the Big Business partner.
- Build independent marketing teams to represent the Big Business partner.
- Teach and mentor others to do the same.

The big business System:

- Compensates *The Little Guy* for both efforts.

...and the most intriguing piece of this revenue- share strategy, the big business:

- Compensates *The Little Guy's* independent marketing team members, allowing each to benefit financially from each other's efforts – *basically, expense free!*

Redirecting part of the profits, money flows through independent, small businesses owned by families and neighbors.

...And just what the hell is wrong with that?

A winner, the consumer, can reap the significant trickle-down rewards of this successful commerce-partnering model. With a brighter bottom-line, the best big businesses can reinvest in better raw materials or more superior services; producing a higher quality consumable and lower prices.

In simplest terms, the big business's challenge is to develop the system to manufacture, inventory and deliver products and services. The task of *The Little Guy* is to connect the big business system to their target market *one-on-one*.

What does it take?

Owning a Systematic Marketing business can be challenging. The same, yet different from traditional business models, the goal in either is to consistently advance the business to the next level of success.

As *The Little Guy*, we get to trash the traditional rules of the work-a-day world. We can find ourselves a leader of leaders versus a hired employee. We can self-schedule our work rather than being driven by preset store hours. Working at our own pace, in our own time, making our own rules, we can *celebrate* our accomplishments, not be *graded by others* on our performance.

If we have chosen wisely, it only takes some rudimentary skills and the belief we can change nothing into something special.

Honing the Skills

Each Systematic Marketing model can require several different skills. Most are little more than the basics we employ every day.

Planning and setting goals: Knowing the next level of success and how we are going to get there.

Networking and meeting people: Making new friends and building relationships; able to hand pick those we want to work with each day.

Training and Coaching: Training others on what we learn and coaching how to use the knowledge; working together to ensure their success.

> **"A candle loses nothing
> When lighting another candle."**

James Keller, Clergyman

Listening to learn: Asking questions of others and *actually* listening; drilling down and determining why others might need what we have to offer.

When asked why others do what they do, most will answer "money"; a very good reason, but not reason enough. Asking probing questions, we find people don't dream of simply winning the lottery. They dream of what they will do with the money when they win!

Developing the Attitude

Systematic Marketing is fertile ground for those with a dream and a *No Matter What!* Attitude.

> *If you want it, you can have it.
> You just have to work for it!*

A deliberate selection for a frame of mind, attitude is a choice as well as a way of life. Our outlook can be positive or negative. We can believe we can or believe we can't. Either way, what we decide will be the truth.

In Systematic Marketing, a positive attitude is at the heart of getting us through the rough patches and will define us as role models.

I believe 20% of life is determined by what happens to me. The other 80% is determined by how I choose to handle what happens to me. I also realize I can only control my attitude; I have no control over that of others.

As someone with a positive frame of mind, we are excited about the possibilities and ready to take action. Keeping an eye on the solution, *not the problem*, we embrace change and don't accept things as they are. Determined to make things the way we want them to be, we are not intimidated by failures and obstacles. Willing to learn, we are coachable and eager for success. We dream the dream and set the goals then check 'em off, *one by one*.

> *"You cannot consistently*
> *Perform in a manner*
> *Which is inconsistent*
> *With the way you see yourself."*

Zig Ziglar, Author, Motivational Speaker

A positive attitude is having a clear vision of the future. Driven to act with purpose and determination, we strive to *see* and *feel* the possibilities; where we want to live, the home we will build, the car we will drive, the balance in our bank account, the perfect vacation, even our retirement.

Ready to lead by example, we will eagerly display our most vibrant attitudes; those so necessary for success.

Optimism: Wallowing in a personal conviction of success.

Hopefulness: Deliberately planting footsteps to reach our goals on the path to our dreams; watching roadblocks turn into stepping stones!

Joy: Relishing the successes of getting where we want to go; savoring the pleasure of pursuing our potential.

Patience: Understanding it takes time to achieve the desired results; knowing our futures can't be built on a get-rich-quick scheme!

Celebration: Taking pleasure in our successes; recognizing and celebrating the accomplishment of others.

Abundance: Forging a path to unlimited, yet equal potential; fueled by optimism and hope.

Generosity: Leading by example; building on the success of others, sharing time and knowledge, helping others grow from where they are to where they want to be.

Appreciation: Recognizing and having gratitude for the good qualities of team members.

Having the Aptitude

Learning: Thirsting for knowledge; open-minded and ready to share what we learn.

Transparency: Being truthful and honest; never exaggerating or embellishing. *If we have chosen wisely,* the truth is more than good enough!

Resolve: Having the tenacity to believe we can succeed.

Commitment: Performing the job at hand, *Doing It On Purpose*, seeking the *Extra-Ordinary*.

Conviction: Being convinced what we have to offer is a good thing; that it has value and can improve lives, ours as well as the lives of others.

We've got it!
They want it!
They just don't know it yet!

Leadership: Being a person of influence; real, fascinated and productive with integrity. Setting the pace, reaching the goals; planning the work and working the plan!

Accountability: Taking responsibility for our mission, our plan, and our dreams.

Working on Self

Self-contentment and complacency are great enemies to personal success and can destroy our plan for the future. As motivated self-starters we are constantly evolving, working on ourselves to grow and thrive.

For things to improve,
I must improve!
For fewer challenges,
I must develop more skills!
For things to get easier,
I must work harder!

Self-confidence: Often, we make statements that are self-limiting instead of asking good, open-minded questions.

Self-Limiting
I can't find a job!
I am not interested!
I'm stuck where I am*!*
What will they think?
I can't!

Open-Minded
How can I earn income?
Hmm! Can this help me?
Is this an option for me?
It's my life, not theirs!
Why not me? Why not now?

Self-belief: Believing in the *power of one;* having the right answers when the inner voice challenges. *Can I really do this? Are others smarter, more deserving than I? What will other people think if I do this? I can't risk failure! Success is for others but not for the likes of me!*

Self can be an internal terrorist
Deftly taking away our power
Simply by whispering softly in our ear!

Self-promise: Keeping our word to ourselves. Perhaps it's a matter of third party accountability?

Self-image: Connecting with others, even when marketing online; putting ourselves out there.

> *"Nobody can make you feel inferior*
> *Without your consent."*

Eleanor Roosevelt, First Lady, Humanitarian

An unshakable self-image will overtake the fear of what other people might think. Challenge the fear by doing it anyway!

Each of us has to determine if the desire for success is stronger than the fear of failure. We *can* move past fear if the worth of the reward is greater than the emotional risk.

Move over: Getting out of our own way; feeling vulnerable, worrying about how we are judged. Sabotaging our self-belief system; the fear of being considered silly or naïve.

If we let it, *fear is a dream killer* and will have us end up living with the results of someone else's thinking - *which is the same as living someone else's life.*

Be coachable: Listen to and emulate the successful.

Focus on the Mission

Our primary mission is to choose the company that has a history and culture that meets our personal beliefs and ethical standards. Then, and only then, should we be willing to invest our time, our energy and our reputation.

The company's products must stir our passions and ignite our energies. By becoming a student as well as customer, we can learn and test and be our own best billboard.

If we choose wisely, we can have the power to dramatically increase our income and plow a high-traffic path for ourselves and others to financial freedom. A clearly defined course will help us succeed at our REAL job; reaching our goals and helping others do the same.

Developing sturdy relationships, we can build and lead an effective team of people with a common goal. On a mission to encourage others to paint *their* vision, we can lead them, taking them where they never thought they could go.

Another important part of our mission is to keep others engaged through education, encouragement, support and celebration; fostering independence by teaching them to teach others to do the same. As leaders-by-example, we develop, communicate, work and duplicate the plan. We are optimistic, enthusiastic and think big. We work hard and have fun, keeping it simple so others can see the possibilities.

Focused on our mission, we can glimpse at the future.

Just imagine...

- The foundation and future of a family raised by both parents, able to be present in the daily lives of their children!

- The impact of family-first on neighborhoods, communities, the nation, the world!
- Being part of, or even the catalyst for, someone else's success!
- Income for a lifetime without risk!

People helping other people succeed. What a concept!

Making the Time

There is good news and bad news! The good news - *we are our own boss*. The bad news - *we are our own boss*.

Unless we are focused, time has a way of slipping by. Each day must be harnessed, deliberately defined by activities and goals.

Killing time isn't murder.
It's suicide!

Everyone is busy. Some are doing busy work; *saddling, not riding*. Some are busy working; *producing results*. The difference is scheduling and calendaring the activities that move our business forward.

Setting the Goals

Something magical happens when pen touches paper. Dreams with realistic goals (not wishes), benchmarks and standards that are written, specific and measurable, will plot our course and gauge our accomplishments.

More than words on paper they are a signature on a contract, evidence of the commitment to ourselves

Goals are a good thing,
As long as they
Don't require a finish line.

If we are (A), our written goals are (B), and our actions are (C); then (A) must be driven by (C) to get to (B) and (B) must be quantifiable, realistic, and attainable.

Does this equation take us where we want to go? If not, one or more factor has to change.

Defining the Plan

Each big business system offers a product and money delivery system based on the company's definition of its work requirements. Each is unique and can produce varying levels of income.

Starting with research, we are challenged to drill down, asking questions until the best fit for our future becomes clear.

Most humans spend more time investigating cell phone plans than researching opportunity.

Success is founded on understanding the requirements, learning what it takes to accomplish them, then developing a step by step plan.

Just imagine...a future based on a deliberate plan; one not lived by default!

Calendaring the Plan

Calendaring action is critical to building a solid, long-term revenue stream. Especially when we are in business for ourselves, we can get lost in the details. Therefore, we must set aside time to commit to the plan, then schedule the actions.

*Listening and learning
Makes us smarter,
Planning and organizing
Makes us prepared,
But it's our actions that
Make us successful!*

Incorporating and detailing a daily calendar is a dependable way to develop and plan strategies. Helping to control our activities, it will point out what is, and isn't, working.

Keeping to a schedule can effectively and efficiently manage time. As a habit, it will provide momentum and reinforce our commitment to personal achievement.

As a dedicated personal assistant, calendaring can alleviate costly memory lapses and be a dependable memory jogger. Helping to identify priorities, it can add value by establishing those activities that will propel us forward.

A reliable and relentless accountability partner, it will constantly challenge the ever-present and resolute enemy of success... *procrastinatio*n.

Working the Plan

Whether an employee, employer or Systematic Marketing business owner, the activities that dictate business growth are much the same.

Become a customer: As our own best customer, we must be willing to set the example by becoming a product of the products.

Create a contact list: This critical element adds possibilities to our customer base. At the heart of our plan, it needs constant attention.

A basic list should include names, phone numbers and e-mail addresses. A more comprehensive list may include their "why"; *what we have learned about what they need simply by listening.*

Prospects for the list are everywhere; family, friends, neighbors as well as new associates we've met at social and business networking events, seminars and lectures. Social media can be a highly effective list-building tool.

In Systematic Marketing, the contact list has an added dimension. It also functions as a list of prospective business partners as well as teammates.

Develop a dialog: When someone asks *"What do you do?"* a general answer should last no more than the time it takes to move between 6 floors (plus or minus 30 seconds) while riding in an elevator, thus the term "elevator speech." The point is to open a dialog, not to give a mini overview.

A more pointed answer would acknowledge something about them or something we both have in common. *"Like you, I am a... business person, a grandparent, a soccer mom."*

Build a relationship: While there is absolutely no excuse to badger or pounce we should always have our antenna up. Asking good questions in a general conversation will help seek out those who are looking for what we have. Honesty is certainly the best policy; no hijacking or planning meetings under false pretenses.

Recruiting people for the sake of recruiting will guarantee a business built on sand.

Fill a need: It's all about them; their goals and their dreams, their "why". Our job is to identify and, *if we can*, fill their need.

If there is no need, there is no lead!

Set an appointment: Setting appointments can be one of the easiest activities to accomplish as long as we:

- Have a constantly refreshed, well-developed contact list.
- Schedule (calendar) time to set appointments.
- Take ownership and believe that the company, its products, and compensation plan are the best any system has to offer.

Whether in person or by phone, be enthusiastic and positive and at the ready to set a date and time. *That's it! Just a date and time.* Keep the conversation simple, short and sweet, no more than a minute or two. Think about how we can make a difference in *their* life.

When calling family or a friend, let them know we've found something important to our future. Perhaps they will see value for themselves. At the very least, ask them to be our cheerleader and accountability partner. Ask for their help.

When calling from a business card, it's about building relationships. Let them know how we came to have their information. If a local contact, mention we are also in business locally. Suggest we might be good referral partners.

Be clear about our intentions for the meeting and always do what we say we will do. Be cheerful, positive, helpful and truthful.

In Systematic Marketing, knowing how to and being comfortable with, making the approach and ultimately setting the appointment is central to our plan for success.

We must cast a line into the water
If we want to catch a fish.

Break the Ice: Starting with a general conversation is a great way to break the ice or renew an acquaintance. Make positive statements, repeat names and ask leading questions to get to know at least one new thing about the person.

"So glad you're here this evening!"
"Did you come straight from work?"
"Did you have to get a sitter?"
"Did you have far to come?"

Tell the story: Telling the story can be a formal presentation or overview offered in person, one-on-one, in groups or online. Whichever, always be the first to arrive. Putting everyone in their comfort zone will help us get to know the "audience" and help them get to know us.

A well-presented overview will include the company's culture, systems and plans for growth as well as the product mix, and the income delivery.

Growing personally and professionally, we are creating our story and how it relates to our company. Others want to know what attracted us to a particular company and what effect it has had on our lives. Sharing this story with posture fueled by pride and conviction will go a long way in making a one-on-one connection with a listener of one or one hundred and one.

Set a professional tone: Remember, *this is a business,* not an excuse for a party! Be respectful. Start and end on time.

Paint the vision: Help others see themselves as successful: reaching their goals.

The listener is favoring us with their time and attention and deserves to see the whole picture and hear how it might relate to them. Be sure to detail how it can benefit *their* bank account and improve *their* lifestyle.

Ultimately, we are asking others to throw in with us as well as the company we have chosen. It is our job to offer the information necessary to help them make an informed decision and assure them of our commitment to their success.

Handle objections: Our human nature tends to gloss over objections, trying to counter with a barrage of positives; a signal we are ignoring or not listening. *Listening to learn,* we can acknowledge their concerns have value and are appreciated. Avoid being argumentative or placing others on the defensive. Recognize there is an objection then follow with good questions until the real reason for the objection becomes clear.

Them: *Oh, I am not interested. This is just one of those!*
Us: OK. I am not sure what you mean by 'one of those?'
Them: *You know, one of those pyramid things.*
Us: I am a little surprised to hear you say that. What do you mean by "pyramid things?"
Them: *Where those at the top get richer, and those at the bottom pay the price!*
Us: Oh, I understand now what you mean. Let me try to help you better understand what we do. I think you might come to a much different conclusion.

Now both parties understand the real objection; "Them," perhaps a little more curious and "Us" more able to address the real objection. Both are now part of a solution-driven conversation. Neither is on the defensive. Confirm there is an agreement, and the objection has been solidly identified and addressed. Don't belabor; move on to the next segment.

Understand the "Yes": "Yes" means we have done our job. It's time to stop talking and seal the deal.

Ask for referrals: Everyone has a circle of influence. Each person we know has a sphere of family, friends, social acquaintances and business associates. *If we ask,* every person has the likelihood to increase our circle of influence. Rather than dealing with a stranger, people prefer to do business with someone they know or someone who has recommended them with a positive endorsement.

I recall having coffee with a prospective client who was really good at asking for referrals. I told him I admired his commitment to the task when he shared his secret.

Although I hadn't noticed, he used an ingrained motion; each time he glanced at his watch, he would be reminded to get back to asking for a referral.

The opportunity for referrals is everywhere and asking for them should be automatic. Make asking a habit that becomes part of our daily conversations. Ask a satisfied customer, a neighbor, another soccer mom or dad, the hairdresser or postman or corner grocery clerk. Always be mindful that referrals can be a two-way street, giving as well as receiving.

Be specific. Identify your target market. *"Do you know anyone who is interested in _____ (fitness, the environment, travel, earning extra income)?"*

Challenging ourselves, we can set referral objectives. Before any event, determine the number of referrals we would like to have and make a personal promise to stay until we succeed. More often than not, we will exceed the challenge!

With these goals, I find I stay longer and meet a lot more people. I also find that asking for referrals produces a more personal conversation and helps to form new relationships.

A referral is a valuable gift and deserves to be treated as such. Take time to send a note or make a phone call expressing gratitude. Let others know we are grateful for the referral as well as their time and trust. Remember to remove the pressure. *"Don't know if this is for you, but I am sure you know people who are looking for what I have to offer."*

Getting good at asking for referrals is our number one business-expansion tool. After our warm market, referrals are our best opportunity. Far more effective than cold calling, referrals can be more productive and certainly less expensive than media marketing and advertising.

Focus on follow-up: Circumstances change! People's needs and dreams shift from day to day, and their goals are written and rewritten constantly. *What if*...we could be there with the possibilities when they do?

Stay in touch with everyone we know especially those who have ever been on our contact list. Continually, reach out to those who have heard our story. Revisit customers, past or present. Check in with those who are working or might have tried to work the business with us in the past. Let them know we are committed to helping them try harder or even start again.

Celebrate success: Success can be a series of small victories, each celebrated as an important step, looking forward to the next. Praise and recognition focused on accomplishment can be motivating and excite others to rise to the occasion.

Lead by example: Make sure our actions as a leader are consistent with our words.

To gain the trust and confidence of those we ask to throw in with us, we must walk the walk; *setting footsteps of success for others to follow* and talk the talk; *doing what we say we will do.*

> *Leaders can take others*
> *Where they never dreamed*
> *They would go!*

Leaders exhibit certain traits, taking them from *Ordinary to Extra-Ordinary.* Among their stand-out traits are truthfulness and honesty and the ability to listen to learn. Courageous and responsible, when necessary, they take the blame and acknowledging failure. Persistent and consistent, they are willing to do the work.   Creative and thoughtful, they are solution-driven to succeed.

Others are watching our every move and want to know by our actions we believe in our success as well as theirs. If they see success because we are taking action; building relationships, scheduling activities, telling our story and growing, so will they. If they trust in our leadership, they will want to emulate our behaviors.

> *Do as I do,*
> *Not just as I say!*

Stay in touch: Company employees are a captive audience able to stay in touch because of their office setting. Systematic Marketing team members are self-governing business owners, each working independently. Daily, at the very least weekly, Systematic Marketing teams should gather in person or by teleconference. Topics for discussion might include planning and training as well as building strength through affirmation and celebration.

Participate in training: We are responsible for our own success.

Good Systematic Marketing companies offer free or affordable training that might include printed materials, seminars, webinars, and mentoring. As independent business owners, it is up to us to take advantage of any training opportunities.

Most successful leaders give generously of their time and experience and are worth listening to and learning from. Our goal is to take the best of what we see and hear, then lead by example, making sure our teams do the same.

The very best way to learn is on-the-job training.

Manage through mentoring: A big part of our job is to be available and helpful. As a mentor, we can get the new business partner started on the right path and stay focused on their "why". Always careful in our actions, teach others to clone what we do and duplicate what they see.

Under-commit and over-deliver: The really good companies are evidence-based and don't need any embellishment or hype.

Be intentional: Doing It On Purpose, taking action, scheduling and planning!

Knowing the purpose

Consider the facts! To make money, someone somewhere has to buy something. This fact doesn't make us pushy or desperate salespeople selling something to someone who doesn't want what we are selling!

If we have chosen wisely and believe in our purpose, we are simply communicators charged with asking relevant questions and, in response, confidently offering pertinent information.

Get over it! We are dealing with difficult challenges including disappointment, criticism, and frustration.

We get in trouble when we:

- *Over-analyze*: Is this worth my time?
- *Lack of conviction:* Why am I doing this?
- *Doubt ourselves:* Can I do this?

...or worse

- *Saddle:* Burning time doing the busy work.

Don't take it personally! Focused on delivering information, we can't be attached to the outcome or the opinion of others. They will "get it" or not.

We will hear LOTS of "No." Learn to love "No." It's the prequel to "Yes." Realistically, most are going to say "No" simply because they can't get out of their own way. They are stuck in the 20th Century, content to be living in others people's thinking.

There is a big difference between saying "No" and rejection. "No" is just "No". Rejection is personal.

"Would you like a cup of coffee?" "No, thank you!" They are saying "No" to the coffee. Don't make it personal.

"Will you marry me?" "No!" Now *that's* personal, having rejected the person.

It's all about them! Each individual's goals and dreams, needs and desires are different. Life is, after all, about having choices.

We can waste precious time trying to convince those who have chosen their path and are not interested in ours. Our job is to sift until we find those who are open to opportunity, are like-minded and want what we have to offer.

Many will join our mission with all good intentions but, *by choice*, will never be successful. It can be disappointing, but we understand we can't want more for others than they want for themselves.

Some Will. Some Won't.
So What? Who's Next?

We will have found our purpose when our days are filled with doing the things we enjoy. To bring our purpose into focus, practice the following:

1. List everything that makes us happy. *A fun exercise in itself!*
2. Highlight the ones that require skill or special talent?
3. Hone that skill or special talent!

Reaching goals can be as simple as loving what we do, then getting good at it! Repetition makes the master!

...and finally, Believe it! Own It! See Systematic Marketing for what it really is!

A Real Shot
At Real Wealth
For The Little Guy

Chapter Four

"I believe an opportunity
To add something good
To another's life is a gift.
...And personally,
I can't wait to give it!"

The Eccentric Influencer

A Numbers Game

Numbers have a way of bottom-lining thoughts and processes.

The 80/20 Rule

Early in the 20th century, Italian economist Vilfredo Pareto created a mathematical formula known today as the **80/20 Rule** or the *Law of the Vital Few*.

This concept, self-titled *Pareto's Principle* was designed to point out the unequal distribution of wealth between the minority and the majority of the people.

For consideration:

80% of businesses share 20% of the revenue
20% of businesses share 80% of the revenue

80% of revenue is from 20% of customers
20% of revenue is from 80% of customers

Over the decades, this theory, *not necessarily a truth*, has become an important business management tool. An effective guideline, it helps bring clarity to complex issues when determining where to focus energy and resources.

It can also be applied when referring to the individual.

80% of the people share 20% of the wealth
20% of the people enjoy 80% of the wealth

Statistically, 80% of the people (employees, employee-preneurs, the self-employed and the small business owner) trade their time and expertise for money and share 20% of the wealth. Conversely, 80% of the wealth is generated by the assets of, and shared by 20% of the people (big business owners, Systematic Marketing CEOs and investors).

In my opinion, to reside on either side of this equation is to be mentally and emotionally different. It's the difference between working hard and working smart.

The Six Principles

The basics of Systematic Marketing:

1. ***Sphere of Influence:***
   Much like ripples in water, our personal sphere extends outward from its core (us). Everyone we know, it includes family, friends, acquaintances, associates and those we serve as well as those who serve our needs. Through our words and actions, we have the power to affect events, influence opinions and even affect the attitude of strangers.

2. **The Power of EnVision:**
    Painting the picture, helping *The Little Guy* imagine the possibilities with them at center stage. Seeing their excitement when they come to understand they have a *real* shot at *real* wealth.

3. **The Art of Duplication:**
    For better or worse, we influence and duplicate by example. Newcomers to our business model know just enough to fail. Our job is to have a simple action plan with well-defined steps that will help them hit the ground running. The ultimate mission is to teach them how to duplicate our actions.

4. **Geometric Growth:**
    A series of mathematical events are set into motion each time we succeed in showing others how to duplicate what we do. As each student becomes the teacher, the rate of duplication or *Geometric Growth* increases.

5. **Leveraging Other People's Time (OPT), Money (OPM) and Effort (OPE):**
    As each new teacher shows the student how to make the best use of their own time, money and effort, the rate of Geometric Growth increases without any upsurge in the teacher's time, money or effort.

6. **Organizational Retention:**
    Maintaining the results of our personal efforts, as well as that of OPT, OPM, OPE, is balanced in the follow-up!

The Seven Components

In Systematic Marketing, there is a variety of companies proclaiming to offer any outsider a way to gain access to, align with, and profit from their internal business system.

Companies can range anywhere from a newly-formed start-up to an established enterprise with an already-proven, successful system. Each has a proprietary business system that includes seven essential components. The very best are deliberately designed to include *The Little Guy*.

1. ***The Company:***
   Most are forward-thinking companies that understand the value of personal-touch marketing. With an appreciation for this unique partnership forged between their systems and *The Little Guy,* the company can see the value of having educated consumers educating others.

2. ***The Management:***
   Systematic Marketing CEOs (*The Little Guys*) and their CEO teams (more *Little Guys*) are independent business owners, managing their own small businesses. Their job is to focus on the activities required by their agreement with their big business partner.

   The big business partner is also an independent business, and their management should function accordingly. Responsible for the company's values and culture, they are also the innovator, researcher, manufacturer, packager, warehouseman, shipper and accountant. Resumes' for their leadership should reflect the individual's experience in managing the big business. Their daily actions should reflect their specific job descriptions.

3. *The Products and Services:*
There is no business without *real* products and services that *real* people want, use and will buy again and again.

The really smart Systematic Marketing business models require each independent subcontractor to be a consumer first. Taking the opportunity, *The Little Guy* can test, evaluate and become educated on the brand and will come to understand the potential impact on each new customer.

4. *The Consumer:*
The end customer is the backbone of any commercial enterprise in any industry and the primary source of revenue and growth.

New customers are expensive to "get". The truly successful companies, traditional as well as Systematic Marketing, know to flourish they must do well to keep those they already have. Fully understanding the importance of customer loyalty, they can gauge their level of success and determine their stability by constantly evaluating their retention rate.

Consumers will remain loyal but only if there is value. In trade for their dollar, they expect and can demand the highest quality at the most reasonable prices supported with the best in customer services.

As owners in Systematic Marketing, we should be our own best customer. After all, if the product or services are something people want, use and buy on a regular basis, why would we not own the business and buy from ourselves?

5. **The Compensation Plan:**
The Compensation Plan is the income or money delivery system. *Studying to choose wisely*, we want the one that takes us where we want to go!

Plans vary widely, most paying for direct sales, purchasing inventory and referrals. Some plans inspire and pay for recruiting. A few pay substantially for simply helping others open customer accounts. The very best plans offer compensation with unlimited income potential.

Complicated compensation plans can be tricky and hard to understand but, as in any business, knowing exactly how money flows to the bottom line, *especially our pockets*, is critical. The Compensation Plan can be the difference between *wanting* to be successful and actually *getting* there.

Benefits, return on investment (ROI), and level of risk are determined by each business model and can be minimal or robust. The level of personal success is mainly dependent on the determination and commitment of *The Little Guy*. The most successful have learned that it's all about leveraging time and resources and understanding geometric growth and duplication.

6. **The Business System**:
 Systematic Marketing business models come in all sizes and structures and probably count in the hundreds.

They have different configurations with "legs" and "columns" and "layers" and "levels". Each structure dictates the various payment percentages, bonuses, and incentives. Several models pay in additional inventory or product sample "kits" and some in products. A handful compensate with tools and equipment. Most pay by company check or direct deposit. Some require pre-purchasing inventory for resale, generating invoices and, on occasion, order delivery. One or two are simple shopping clubs with coupons and discounts and rebates.

7. **The Little Guy:**
 Most are content working hard for others with the belief they have limited risk or personal liability. Challenged to find the perfect job, they are willing to trade their time and efforts for the benefits, security and stability of a steady paycheck.

Some are focused on running their small business enterprises willing to risk and accept personal liability. Most are traditional thinkers, happiest living in their familiar zones. Perhaps for their needs, *they have chosen wisely.*

Then, there are those who are ready to tackle a different set of challenges. Anxious to be cut from the herd, each strives to work smarter, hoping to produce vastly different results.

Challenges, for the most part, are personal, therefore, can be controlled. Meeting these challenges puts us in charge; able to control the outcome.

Chapter Five

"Lucky breaks come by chance. Success comes by choice."

John Addison
Leadership Editor, *Success*

Success is a Choice

The prosperous and well-informed earn their power by the actions they choose to take based on the knowledge and understanding they gain through study and investigation.

The less informed have a tendency to base their choices on the missed opportunities of others. Some rely on hearsay and some choose to live inside other people's thinking. Much like old wives' tales, these observations can be shortsighted, outdated and at great personal cost.

Many Systematic Marketing business systems are similar, but no two is exactly alike. Each company has a unique compensation plan and can cover a wide spectrum; paying for direct sales or kicking back a percentage of inventory purchases. Some inspire and pay for referrals and some encourage and pay for recruiting. Many are complicated and can be tricky making them difficult to understand. The simpler, the better!

The objective is to distinguish the *really, really good* from the *not-so-good* and expose the *really, really ugly*. With cautious assessment, there is something for everyone. It's about choosing the right one; the plan that takes us where we want to go.

The Really, Really Good

Only a handful of companies offers limitless possibilities with true residual income and equal opportunity.

The best are blind to age or level of education and care nothing for race or gender or our personal history of success or failure.

Worth-our-investigation companies have an easy-to-understand marketing, distribution, and compensation plan.

The exceptional plans don't require large sums of money or significant inventory if any at all. Some are based on selling; some require minimal inventory and some entail personal product delivery. A few are all about gaining new customers and customer retention.

The most reputable produce legitimate products and sought-after services. Designed around high-quality, high-demand, value-priced consumables, they answer the consumers need for ongoing services.

Those companies who believe world-class service is a priority, purposely position the customer as part of the overall organization. Retention remains high when the customer can experience the "feel" of being part of something important.

Marketing is generally by word-of-mouth but can include some traditional marketing strategies. Companies with the highest potential income plans are built on marketing teams made up of members and their partners enjoying personal success by way of helping each other become successful.

Well-structured systems pay handsomely for person-to-person marketing, compensating families and communities rather than retailers.

A+ companies offer sustainable, long- term residual income with minimal or no risk. Really good at what they do, they also recognize that compensating and rewarding professional behaviors help to endorse their commitment to excellence.

If chosen wisely, a Systematic Marketing business is free of employees and overhead, and in most cases, there is no inventory or selling or collections or deliveries.

The Not-So-Good

Many of these companies sell non-consumables or expensive services that can strain family budgets. When a family is challenged financially, these items are the first to be canceled.

Owning a business in Systematic Marketing should be simple, not to be misunderstood as easy. Companies with complicated plans make them difficult to understand what it takes to be successful. The most effective steps are not clearly defined or quantified.

Each member is a part of a distribution chain with the opportunity to buy-in with an initial investment that can be significant. In exchange, the member receives products or services at different levels of wholesale cost determined by the dollar amount of their investment. When sold, the markup then becomes the member's profit or source of income.

As marketers, each can be paid a percentage of the buy-in when recruiting others to do the same. The ongoing product or services pricing is determined by a variety of factors including the rank or level of participation.

Some expect members to pre-buy inventory at wholesale and constantly maintain stock for resale; ever ready to take orders, make deliveries and collect the profit. Again, their income is based on a markup; mostly to their friends and family.

Great! Now we have bought a job selling stuff to make money at the expense of our friends and family. Isn't this simply paying to have a job; selling products or services without a guaranteed paycheck?

A few are designed without distributors or multiple levels of distribution. Members are expected to make an initial investment in exchange for pricey "sales" or "demonstration" kits so they can host pricey parties and offer demonstrations using the contents of the "kits." Kit ingredients must be replenished at the member's expense.

Some expect members to take orders in person or publish a code, asking their customers (if they remember) to use the code when placing their order online.

Is this where the badgering begins?

Many companies encourage the membership to profit from the sale of a wide range of expensive sales support materials to their teams, such as presentation binders, CDs, forms and other promotional materials.

A majority of these companies charge extra fees, often in significant amounts, when a member chooses to be more than a customer and decides to participate in the business plan. Encouraged by their leadership to tout big checks and make substantial payout claims, they are forbidden to reveal the overall income statistics or the company's gross sales.

A good many plans separate the customers, isolating them from the general organization making them ineligible to participate in the organizational product and money delivery system. The theory behind this practice is to save money by only paying a commission to the "enroller" on the customer's purchases.

By separating the customers from the business builders takes away a team customer service concept, leaving the customer to fend for themselves. The smart companies are beginning to understand this is marketing suicide, not only for the customer but also for the company. This foolishness discourages and dilutes attention to the customer and, in turn, puts the customer at risk.

There are those who encourage product loading (buying more even if we don't need it!) and offer advancement (maybe lower prices or higher bonuses or better compensation percentages) based on the company's product sales rather than the success of the teams. Worse, they encourage each member to encourage their teams to do the same.

In my experience, any business model based on product loading doesn't work in the long term.

Instead of building on the successes of others, these companies take advantage of the member's time, money, effort as well as their personal reputation.

The Really, Really Ugly

Most border on the illegal with plans just to skate by. Most two-legged "binary" plans restrict growth, reward lethargy and promote entitlement. Famous for limiting income, they are deliberately set up for failure. Structured to take advantage of the trusting and the vulnerable, they use careful language to hide the bad stuff.

The product is not important. It's simply a signup game, recruiting without any interest or regard for the individual.

Some allow the *bleedership* (management) to own a downline (a competing organization). When charged with deciding what's best for the company, the *bleedership* will usually promote and endorse a personal, rather than a business, outcome.

Quite a few claim to offer residual income but make it impossible to advance. Constructed so the revenue always goes to the top, the last in can never make more than the first.

They might include breakaways (exactly what it sounds like) designed to remove the successful from the business organization of those who sponsored them initially. The *really* sneaky claim the sponsor doesn't deserve to benefit because they didn't do 100% of the work.

Well, who trained them by example, held their hand when they were frustrated and talked them out of it when they were ready to quit? Who was responsible for bringing these newly successful to the company in the first place?

Many plan these business systems around hype and hyperbole, designed to ride a temporary wave; getting in, making money and getting out, leaving others holding the bag.

Among the worst are those who hold the member hostage by offering bonuses up front with the expectation of payback. Car bonuses are common in most plans but differ drastically in the fine print. Only a handful reimburse payments on a regular basis. The *really* ugly promote buying expensive, designer cars and promise reimbursement as long as the member "holds status." Should the member drop out of status, reimbursements might not start again for at least one year.

Choosing Wisely

Mistakenly, many of us begin our Systematic Marketing careers because a friend has recommended a particular company. That's fine, but the referral is only a starting point.

The key to finding real success is to *choose wisely*. It takes **Doing It On Purpose**; devoting time to drill down and ask the difficult questions. We are contemplating a business venture that could affect the rest of our lives. Even though tedious at times, the goal is to find *THE ONE* that incites our passion for its products and ignites our drive for *extra-ordinary* financial success.

The best, most lucrative plans are the simplest; requiring the least work, the lowest investment or entry fee, the smallest monthly commitment and the least risk. Plans with the highest reorder and retention rates produce the quickest and highest returns.

In the end, the information gathered will help discover which will best fit with our personality, our skills and especially our goals. We will be ready to bet our money, time, effort, reputation and especially our future - but only *if we have chosen wisely*.

The Evaluation

The following exercise is meant to be a research tool. Each question is intended to be thought-provoking, helping to discover pertinent details about *The Seven Components* in each prospective company.

A free Companion Worksheet is available to help track each answer and present an overall picture. By adding columns to the Worksheet, several companies can be evaluated at the same time.

Worksheet answers should be obvious or at the very least, readily available through the potential sponsor, enroller or a company representative. A "Yes" answer is preferred; a "No" could be a deal breaker or just a signal to dig deeper. Some questions are deliberately duplicated and some may not apply.

Download the Companion Worksheet by following the link at:

http://www.theeccentricinfluencer.com/#!thetools/gf9l0

The Company

1. *Is there published information readily available for research on the company?* Financially, ethically, legally?
2. *Is it stable?* How long has the company been in business? If the answer is less than five (5) years, dig deeper.
3. *Is it well funded?* What is their cash flow picture? Perform a credit rating check!
4. *Are they consistently increasing revenue and reporting steady advancement and growth?* Do their progress charts indicate positive and consistent growth?
5. *Do they have a good income-to-debt ratio?* Take a look at the company's financials and understand their profit picture. Are they debt free?
6. *Do they have a positive legal history?* Has the company had to defend itself against any consumer complaints? Have the results been positive or negative for the company?
7. *Do they have comprehensive and well-defined Mission, Values and Vision Statements that are published and available for examination?* Always, the devil is in the details!
8. *Are they the original manufacturer or services provider?* Have they invested in assets such as machinery and equipment? Are they just an aggregator or reseller; a middleman with no investment?

9. *Is their revenue based mainly on the sale of products and services?* Is the most significant portion of their income based on the sale of expensive proprietary marketing or training tools?

10. *Do they have a professional website?* What is the website address? Is it professionally detailed?

11. *Do they enjoy a professional reputation?* Do they have a good name held in high esteem by their customers and affiliates?

12. *Have they earned awards for accomplishment?* Good companies are visible for the right reasons as well as the wrong. Research to understand their accomplishments and awards as well as their weaknesses and flaws.

13. *Are they a member of a credible industry association?* The Direct Selling Association (DSA)?

14. *Would I deal with this company even if I didn't have an opportunity to make money?* Would I be a loyal customer without the business opportunity?

The Management

15. *Do they have business management experience?* Are they proficient in managing the day-to-day business?

16. *Have the core leaders managed this company for more than five years?* Have they left and started new companies in the same industry? If so, why?

17. *Do they publish their resume' or work history?* What are their accomplishments? Do they have published job descriptions?

18.   *Are they forbidden to own and manage a competing "downline"? Are they paid on product production or services management? Are they making decisions for the company or their personal pockets?*

19.   *If I had a company, would I hire this management team?* Would I trust this team with my time, resources and reputation?

The Products and Services

20.   *Is the product/services mix varied?* How many items does the company supply and do they cover a broad spectrum for the consumer?

21.   *Are they unique proprietary, patented, patent pending?* Can they be purchased only through the members? Companies should not take orders directly without crediting the referring member.

22.   *Are they of high quality?* Does the supplier use high-quality ingredients and monitor its supply chain for the same?

23.   *Are they in demand?* Something customers need, want and are willing to pay for?

24.   *Are they consumable?* Used on an ordinary basis over a continuous period? If changing our financial picture is the primary goal, our choice of companies should be first and foremost, based on products that are consumable. Critical to establishing a stable income stream, product orders should constantly be renewed and purchased on a consistent basis.

25.   *Are they affordable?* Are prices competitive with retail and online stores? Can the consumer buy at wholesale prices?

26.   *Are they effective?* Market-tested and proven to work?

27.   *Do they bring value?* Do they make a difference?

28. *Are they recession proof?* Do consumers need them, no matter what?

29. *Is the pricing the same for all customers?* Some companies have different price structures for different levels of participation. Committed customers should be able to buy at wholesale.

30. *Are customers loyal to the brand?* What is the customer retention rate?

31. *Do the products/services have a high reorder rate?* Do customers buy the products on a consistent basis?

32. *Have new items been launched in the past year?* Are they cutting edge or built on gimmicks rather than sound business principles?

33. *Do they offer coupons and specials?* Loyal consumers deserve special treatment.

34. *Is there a quality guarantee or warranty?* What is the replacement, refund or return policy?

35. *Would I buy and use the product/services even if I couldn't make money?* Are they worthy to be my first choice?

The Consumer

36. *Am I a part of the company's target market?* Who is their target market?

37. *Is consumer labeling clear and comprehensive?* Is product quality as good as, or better than traditional retail outlets?

38. *Will the consumer get a good deal?* Are prices comparable or less expensive than retail?

39. *Is pricing the same for the consumer and the business builder?* Can goods be purchased wholesale by all levels of membership?

40. *Adding in the cost of delivery, are the products/service still a good deal?* Are the delivery methods speedy and affordable?

41. *Can orders be placed online?* Many of today's consumers are online shoppers.

42. *Does the company provide exceptional customer service?* With so many shopping options, today's savvy consumer expects above average customer services.

43. *Am I willing to be a customer?* Are the products/services something I need, want and will pay for?

44. *Can I just be a customer?* Do I have to work the business? Watch for price variances! Some companies charge extra to have access to the business-building piece.

The Compensation Plan

45. *Is the income plan viable, lucrative, and dependable?* Is the plan workable as well as financially rewarding and reliable? Is compensation fair and generous?

46. *Does company policy dictate the percentage of the company's profit set aside to pay its members?* Is this information disclosed publically? Does the company publish statistics about earnings and member's success ratios?

47. *Is the entry fee minimal and affordable?* Is it something in which *The Little Guy* can afford to invest?

48. *Is compensation a product of the products?* What is compensation based on? Direct sales? Recruiting? Customer activity? The really good companies are based on a *lot* of customers purchasing a *little* each month?

49. *Is the plan truly residual?* Understanding that "residual" means doing something once and getting paid over and over.

50. *Is financial growth sustainable independent of effort?* Can an individual member benefit from the efforts of the team?

51. *Are there achievable bonuses, monthly promotions, and incentives?* Review the fine print for possible payback demands or limited reimbursements.

52. *Is the income unlimited and significant?* Is it without caps or limits? Can it grow to be a life changing income?

53. *Is the business model sustainable?* Is the income built on products/services that are in demand and consumable?

54. *Is it truly an equal opportunity?* Do all members have the same opportunity to reach their financial goals? Is there equal opportunity to advance?

55. *Can a team member surpass the person who introduced them to the company?* In rank and income?

56. *Is advancement based on the success of others?* What does it take to advance? Different income levels are determined by personal leadership and team success. Some are based on dollars invested in inventories.

57. *Does the plan incent the kind of behavior I agree with?* Does it encourage team building and reward hard work? Some reward complacency and foster the wrong activities.

58. *Do the successful stay in the enroller's income stream or are they placed elsewhere?* As team members become successful, do they become a "breakaway" business and move outside the enroller's organization?

59. *Is the personal production requirement low?* As a consumer, is the ongoing monthly requirement sustainable?

60. *Are there any extra spiffs?* Car bonus? If so, what is required to earn the bonus but more important, what are the requirements to maintain the rights to the bonus?

61. *Does the company prohibit product loading to advance and earn bonuses?* Specifically, what do I have to do to increase my level of financial success?

62. *Do they have a good compensation record?* What is the company's history of paying compensation? Do they pay on time? Are they accurate? Do they take unauthorized fees or make unauthorized deductions?

63. *Are payments to old/new members based on the same effort?* If the job is the same, the payment should be the same. Bonuses may vary.

The Business

64. *Is the initial investment affordable?* Does it cost extra if I decide to build the business? Some companies require a minimum fee to be a customer with an additional investment to work the business model.

65. *Are all fees clearly defined?* Are there any arbitrary fees that provide no apparent value? Some companies require upfront fees that promise value but only if the new member is successful.

66. *Are the inventory requirements clearly defined?* Some companies require the member to invest in their products for resale or inventory. Many companies trade a "starter" inventory for the

initial investment and require stocking and selling. A few simply require the member to be a customer.

67. *Is the personal monthly product production requirement clearly defined?* Companies should require each member to be a customer of their products and services. Product knowledge and first-hand experiences are necessary for credibility.

68. *Are any required business expenses well defined?* Is there any overhead expense? Typically, members work from home without employees. If there is any overhead, it should be minimal.

69. *Is the plan risk-free?* Is there a financial risk? How much is invested therefore at risk?

70. *Is it a workable money delivery system?* Does it promote exponential growth?

71. *Is advancement based on the success of others?* Is it based on a team working together toward a common goal?

72. *Can customers place orders directly with the company?* Do I have to take orders? Some still do although, with the popularity of online purchasing, most offer the option for the customer to place their orders directly with the company.

73. *Does the factory ship directly to the end customer?* Do I have to sell products? Most do require sales or at the least a "guaranteed" production of points based on personal purchases or the "groups" purchases.

74. *Does the company invoice customers and collect money?* Most models accept direct payment by credit card online.

75. *Is there an acceptable retention rate?* What is the customer retention rate, month over month?

76. *Does the plan include customers in the business organization?* Some only allow business builders to work with business builders, separating the general customer base from the main organization.

77. *Is compensation based on customer purchases?* What is the business builder's primary source of revenue? Is compensation based on the sale of products/services or on recruiting others?

78. *Does the company's website serve both member and customer?* Am I required to have a personal website? Does the company require I invest in a company-approved website?

79. *Do they offer company training and support?* Free or affordable? On-on-one corporate coaching?

80. *Is the business willable, transferable or available for sale?* After years of hard work, is this business something I can treat as a legacy?

81. *Does the plan incent the kind of behavior I agree with?* Ethically and financially?

The Little Guy

If given the choice, would you be:

- An employee: Starting over at zero each week; paid by others to work on behalf of *their* goals and dreams?
- A traditional business owner: Starting over each month, paying others to work on behalf of *your* goals and dreams?
- A Systematic Marketing business owner; *Paid by others* to work on behalf of *your* goals and dreams.

Most answers may seem obvious but not so for the many who don't understand the realism of the choices. For most, their loftiest dreams are limited by their job description, their financial responsibilities or the never-ending demands on their time.

The question is, ***will my choice give me unlimited access to my wildest dreams?***

Critical to the successful development of your Systematic Marketing business is knowing the why of your "why." Why would you buy a lottery ticket? To win, of course! But why do you want to win? It's what you will *do* with what you win is your real "why".

82. *Do I know my "why"? Why am I considering a Systematic Marketing business? The answer is never money; it's the reason for the money.*

83. *Am I prepared to calendar my activities?* How much time will I set aside each week to dedicate to my success? Part time or full time? The really good companies *are not* centered on a get-rich-quick deal. As in any business, it takes serious commitment to be successful.

84. *Do I have well-defined, written goals?* Our destination is determined by a journey well-planned with well-defined short and long term goals.

85. *Will the system I choose take me where I want to go?* If our destination and journey don't match, one or the other has to change.

86.   *Would I use the products or services if I didn't choose to build the business?* Do I believe in, and have a passion for, the company's culture and products?

87.   *Am I willing to be accountable?* We can easily be derailed when working from home.

88.   *Am I coachable?* Success leaves clues. Don't work to reinvent the wheel. Seek out and emulate those who are successful.

89.   *Am I a self-starter?* Am I committed to being persistent, dedicated and consistent?

90.   *Am I prepared to team up, working in sync with a team with a common goal?* Am I ready to get and stay excited and motivated with team calls, texts and emails?

91.   *Am I convinced I can't hurt anyone financially or ethically in my quest to reach my goals?* Will I be comfortable, *even proud*, to represent this company?

Chapter Six

"I've learned that people will forget what you said, people will forget what you did, but people will never forget how you made them feel."

Maya Angelou, Poet

Doing It On Purpose

A brilliant, but much-misunderstood income model, Systematic Marketing is misjudged for a most *usual* reason... **it sounds too good to be true.**

Driven by technology, especially the reach of the Internet, the *really, really* good Systematic Marketing companies have successfully shaken off the checkered past of their ancestors. Led by a handful of well-founded ethical companies, each is working hard to push aside those with less-than-ethical intentions.

The best are original equipment manufacturers (OEM) rather than a value-added reseller (VAR). The most successful are focused on developing and providing in-demand, consumable products and services.

Marketing is driven by innovative programs that offer partnership opportunities with compensation plans centered on a revenue- share strategy. As partners, *The Little Guy* can earn a share of the big business's revenues by representing the company; reaching out to and growing a loyal customer base, *person-to-person*.

The best of the best have developed partner compensation plans that are founded on repeat customer sales creating residual income; *getting paid over and over for doing something once.*

Who's in Charge?

Starting from scratch, *The Little Guy* can benefit from a business plan that builds on itself. Earnings are based *continually* on yesterday's efforts, not constantly starting over again each week or month. Unlike earning linear income, *trading time for money*, residual income can be stable and reliable and will continue to pay out long after the initial effort has passed.

Residual question: What's better, earning a one-time payment of $500.00 or being paid $100.00 a month for the rest of our life?

Fact: A million dollars in the bank earning 6% interest would produce about $60,000.00 annually before taxes.

The question is...got a million dollars?

...and there's more! Instead of Uncle Sam taxing every penny of our income, he becomes an active partner giving us tax breaks and incentives to help us succeed. *(See your tax advisor for details.)*

With the technology of the internet, cell phones, and tablets, our Systematic Marketing income is portable offering flexible lifestyle choices. It can be dependably profitable whether managed on the road, on vacation, at home or even in another city or country.

No matter what, to earn income we still have to show up for work every day. Commitment to specific hours to perform specific tasks will help ensure we reach our specific, predetermined goals. The difference is in the answer when we ask ourselves:

- Who sets the hours? *We do!*
- Who defines the tasks? *We do!*
- Who determines the goals? *We do!*

The Common Goal

What if it were really true...

- We could hand-pick the people we work with every day?
- We could be an equal part of a team of everyday people focused on a common goal?
- We could work together, each doing a little, not just a handful of talented people doing a lot?

As systematic partners pulling together, we can team up to generate significant individual income to put back into our communities.   Able to be participants in our local economy, we are no longer just recycling our dollars through retail chains and big box stores.

Teams are formed by exponential growth based on duplication. Each member contributes to and benefits from the success of the other. Eventually, Individual long-term businesses begin to take shape with *The Little Guy* as CEO. Each is compensated for personal efforts as well as on the efforts of the teams they build.

Those CEOs with the most success exist and thrive by supporting, encouraging and celebrating each other.

The objective is to form new teams of other *Little Guys*; all focused on connecting big business and its goods directly to the consumer. The big business, in turn, redirects a large portion of its significant marketing and advertising dollars back to the teams.

Our support team is compensated on our success, and we earn commissions to help others. ALL are compensated by the big business partner!

Let me get this straight...someone pays me to build a team of people who are paid by someone else - then pays me on their efforts, too?

...And just what the hell is wrong with that?

With an opportunity to live the dream, *The Little Guy* begins to reap the rewards of aggregating and leveraging other people's expertise (OPE), other people's money (OPM) and other people's time (OPT).

Leverage question: What's better... earning a one-time payment of $500.00 or 5% of the efforts of others for the rest of our life?

In a Nutshell

There are only two ways to generate income. Neither is right nor wrong.

1. *Self-at-Work:*
   Income earned by expending personal time and expertise.

2. Assets-at-Work:

Revenue earned from resources that continually regenerate income.

We can...

Work for the system: We are hired by others to be *self-at-work;* trading time and expertise for money. Expending *our* labor on *their* time.

Own the System: We are business innovators accepting the risk and ongoing expense; *self-at-work* working for and owning an *asset-at-work*. Expending *our* labor on *our* time.

Buy into the System: We are license or franchise owners; self-at-work paying to work for the system. *Purchasing* the right to expend *our* labor on *our* time.

Access the System: We are Systematic Marketing CEOs, tapping into an established asset; creating an *asset-at-work*. Assets are expending labor on *our* behalf, *all the time.*

Invest in the System: We are investors, betting our money on the system. Creating an *asset-at-work* that creates other *assets-at-work* on *our* behalf, *all the time.*

Chapter Seven

*"Fear is the
Apprehension of the unknown.
The unknown is
A lack of knowledge.
Therefore, knowledge
Is the cure for fear."*

The Eccentric Influencer

Ordinary to Extra-Ordinary

We, as humans, think and feel and are driven by reason, which can work for or against us. We all want the same things; *the good life with good health, wealth, and affection.*

We see vivid examples through television personalities, the media and even through the lifestyles of our neighbors and friends.

For some of us, our shortfall is worrying what others will say and find ourselves living in other people's thinking; *for better or for worse.*

We *see* and *want* but really feel as though there are but a few choices. We simply don't believe in ourselves or our abilities. We love *our comfort zones*, which really should be called our *familiar zones.*

Frustrated, we believe we have little hope or opportunity to live among the 20% who enjoy 80% of the wealth. With a fear of the different, we abhor risk and avoid any chance of failure.

Wanting rather than *doing,* we are content to live in frustration, reasoning that we have to accept life as *'it is what it is.'* Our dreams and goals are now fuzzy and out of sync with our actions.

A great many of us are content with our journey and confident in our future. We are satisfied with our lifestyle, our job, and our income.

The Value of an Open Mind

Then, there are those of us who are willing to learn and eager to take a chance. We are open to the unorthodox and the non-traditional. Planners and achievers, we are the want-mores and the show-me-how's. Calculated risk-takers, we seek the independence and financial freedom earned by the 20%.

The mind is like a parachute,
It only works when it is open.

Anthony J. D'Angelo
Author

A New Mindset

This new age does bring a different set of challenges and requires a mind reset especially for the last century conformist.

As a 21st Century non-conformist, we are a bit of a rebel; a positive spirit always at the ready to test fresh opportunities. An information-seeker and a mold-breaker, we make decisions based on knowledge, living comfortably in our own thinking.

The Systematic Marketing industry is jam-packed with non-conformists; those who ask,

What if...it were really true, The Little Guy could earn a stable, lifetime income simply by riding the coattails of an already-established, market-proven business system?

What if...it were really true, The Little Guy could own a highly successful business by being part of a team working together toward a common goal?

What if...it were really true, The Little Guy could work from home, prioritized by family first?

What if...it were really true, The Little Guy could make all the money ever needed by helping others reach their financial goals?

What if...it were really true, The Little Guy could do all this without suffering other people's risk or liability?

What if...it were really true, The Little Guy could have a *real* shot at *real* wealth?

Seeking the power of knowledge, we can quickly come to understand we have a realistic opportunity to have a more-than-our-share slice of the good life.

Suspect because it breaks with tradition, Systematic Marketing is an ever-evolving commerce model that has proven to change lives emotionally, physically and especially financially. Offering unlimited income for authentic financial freedom, it can be a way of life with family first.

If we choose wisely, Systematic Marketing screams freedom from debt and eradicating risk and scoffs at working for the man. Promising to be out-of-step, it smacks of the non-traditional offering a new perspective. Packed with potential, it's filled with time and independence and an equal chance for a level playing field.

It beckons to those who want it all not afraid to go against the grain and willing to work hard. Begging to be understood, it knows it can change lives. It is wide open for the curious, the open-minded, the knowledge-hungry and the possibility seekers.

Those of us who want more are beginning to see a different place for ourselves. When we truly understand the startling possibilities offered in Systematic Marketing, we are often surprised by the facts... *It does require hard work but for a minimal investment, it offers low risk and high-income potential.*

Learning that leads to knowledge
= Smart
Learning that leads to action
= Rich

As employees in a traditional business, levels of success (meeting the company's goals) might be compensated by raises and promotions determined by others. As CEO of a Systematic Marketing system, the levels of success are simply *The Little Guy's* next goal waiting to be accomplished.

Now, *entirely within our control*, we no longer have to ask for our rewards. They are there, waiting for us to claim them as our own. They are there simply for the taking. The timing is up to us.

Lost and Found

Are we lost forever in the thinking of others or are we ready to find our perfect fit, *the one path that takes us where we dream to go*?

We need only to believe we have...

A Real Shot
At Real Wealth
For The Little Guy!

The Promise

I solemnly vow never to be complacent again! Today, I have forgiven myself the lack of curiosity, the absence of open-mindedness and the acceptance of the ordinary. I am finished with reacting to the needs of just getting by.

I have overlooked the consequences of all those years spent following the crowd. I promise to live no longer in other people's thinking and giving others a say-so. I will lead my life by design, with intent, no longer by default. I will courageously leave my safe and innocuous familiar zone so that I may live prosperously in my exciting and exhilarating comfort zone.

I am committed to **Doing It On Purpose** by exploring the possibilities. I strive to set the example and encourage others, especially *The Little Guy,* to be *extra*-ordinary; to take charge and have the courage to stop living in the thinking of others.

I understand my every thought, every footstep, my every word marks the passage of my lifetime. I still have a long way to grow and so much yet to do; so much yet to share.

Could it be God isn't finished with me just yet?

Coming Soon...

A New Series

By
The Eccentric Influencer

Doing It On Purpose

Executing a deliberate,
Proactive deed,
Determined by a specific plan,
Performed with the resolve and commitment,
To achieve an intended goal...
No Matter What!

...Ordinary to Extra-Ordinary

Ordinary people
Doing Extra-Ordinary things!

The
Doing It On Purpose
...Ordinary to Extra-Ordinary
Series

...is a collection of attitudes and aptitudes learned and earned by many years of first-hand experiences.

The series includes an assortment of diverse yet related topics; each explored and exposed by *The Eccentric Influencer* from a real-world, rather than a speculative or theoretical point of view.

One at a time, each topic revisits the past, analyzing and assessing, helping to develop the present; always listening to learn while shaping the future.

Each might step out of bounds or push the limits but promises the wisdom and insight born of decades of experience and the hindsight that comes with age.

The Authors Profile

Although a child of the universe, *The Eccentric Influencer* was born to a family of passionate entrepreneurs and obsessive dreamers.

Some were frustrated architects of their own daydreams, and some were passionate creators, inventors, and visionaries. Some were good at business and some simply idealists.

Proven to be thinkers and analysts, they were remarkable problem-solvers seriously seeking solutions. Asking good questions, they pursued the *consistent* answer and constantly colored outside the lines.

Stumbling in the footsteps of her ancestry, *The Eccentric Influencer* has gained invaluable insight as an industry pioneer and forerunner. Working tirelessly to grow and to learn, she rose to meet and conquer the challenges of corporate leadership.

Maturing as a vision-driven innovator, she became an optimistic and enthusiastic entrepreneur. As founder and Chief Executive Officer for several businesses, both large and small, *The Eccentric Influencer* has eagerly learned the bittersweet lessons taught by success as well as failure.

As decades have passed, her role as an entrepreneur has taken on a different look and feel. Less about chasing the dream, it has become more about legacy and her passion to share.

Through the pen as well the podium, *The Eccentric Influencer* offers hindsight, generously sprinkled with intimate insight gathered specifically for those *more than eager* to become... *extra*-ordinary.

Making Contact

To reach the Eccentric Influencer, arrange for speaking engagements or for further information on this book or others in the upcoming series...

Website: **TheEccentricInfluencer.com**

Facebook: The Eccentric Influencer

E-Mail: **info@TheEccentricInfluencer.com**

Write: The *Eccentric Influencer*
c/o GreeneLink Consulting
Post Office Box 698
Flagler Beach, FL 32136

Phone: 386.243.5313